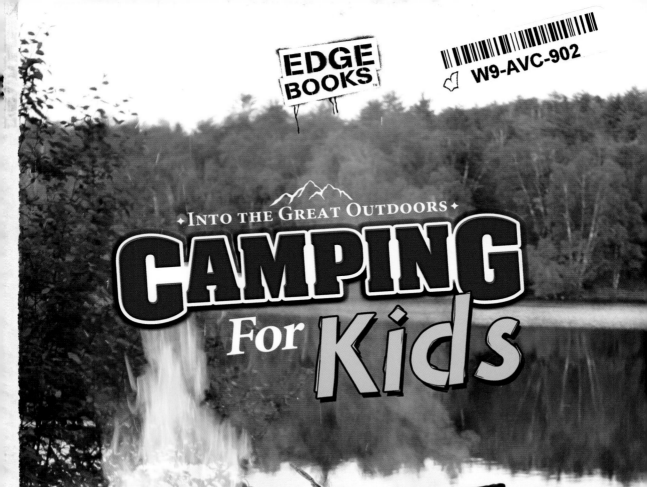

✦ INTO THE GREAT OUTDOORS ✦

CAMPING For Kids

BY MELANIE A. HOWARD

Consultant:
Gabe Gassman
Backcountry Operations Supervisor
Lamar River District
Yellowstone, Wyoming

CAPSTONE PRESS
a capstone imprint

Edge Books are published by Capstone Press,
1710 Roe Crest Drive, North Mankato, Minnesota 56003.
www.capstonepub.com

Library of Congress Cataloging-in-Publication Data
Howard, Melanie A.
Camping for kids / by Melanie A. Howard.
p. cm. — (Edge books. into the great outdoors)
Includes bibliographical references and index.
Summary: "Explores the popular activity of camping, including tips,
techniques, conservation, and specific gear needed"—Provided by publisher.
ISBN 978-1-4296-8423-1 (library binding)
ISBN 978-1-4296-9266-3 (paperback)
ISBN 978-1-62065-224-4 (ebook PDF)
1. Camping—Juvenile literature. I. Title.
GV192.2.H68 2013
796.54083—dc23
                                    2012004671

Editorial Credits
Lori Shores, editor; Ted Williams, designer; Marcie Spence,
    media researcher; Laura Manthe, production specialist

Photo Credits
Alamy: Pep Roig, 26, Tom Bean, 29; iStockphoto: MrsVega, 25, YanC,
4-5; Shutterstock: ChipPix, 6 (inset), Chrislofoto, 24, Dannay, 22, Flashon
Studio, 1, Galyna Andrushko, 8, 11, Iwona Grodzka, 14, Kapu, 3, Karl R.
Martin, 16-17, Kiselev Andrey Valerevich, 13, maga, 6-7, Maslov Dmitry,
10, Mat Hayward, 18, Studio1One, cover, Warren Goldswain, 21

For Grandpa, with love from your fishin' buddy.

Printed in the United States of America in North Mankato, Minnesota.
122013   007949R

TABLE OF CONTENTS

CHAPTER 1

OUT IN THE WILD

Grandpa and Mel stood on a rock just offshore of the campsite. The wind was just strong enough to keep the mosquitoes away. Only the clap of the small waves, rustling leaves, and the call of a loon broke the silence.

One by one the stars appeared. Soon thousands of twinkling lights filled the sky. The moonlight shimmered on the water. Grandpa and Mel felt like the only two people in the world.

"This is why I come out here," Grandpa said quietly.

Mel nodded. "Me too."

FACT
Always be sure to tell someone where you are going when you leave for a camping trip. Also let someone know when you plan to be home.

Getting Out

Campers have been enjoying nature's wonders for more than 100 years. Camping for fun started in the late 1800s. The first campgrounds in North America sprang up in the 1920s. These parks and **preserves** help to protect nature and people by setting rules for safety and **conservation**.

Camping became more popular after World War II (1939–1945). Families had more free time. They had cars that could get them out of town. Camping quickly became the family activity so many enjoy today.

preserve—a place where animals can live and be protected from hunters

conservation—the protection of valuable things, especially forests, wildlife, and natural resources

People are creative when it comes to camping. Some people camp on bicycle trips, strapping their gear to their bikes. Others pile into a recreational vehicle (RV) and target RV campsites. People often camp on hiking trips. You can also boat or snowmobile to a campsite. If there is a way to get you into the wild, you can add camping to your adventure.

FACT
More than 280 million people visited national parks in 2010.

CHAPTER 2

PACKED UP AND READY TO GO

Camping is all about making good use of limited space. You probably won't have room to bring your TV into the wilderness. Essentials include food, water, and shelter. Flashlights are important at night, and sunscreen is just as important during the day. Maps and a compass or a **GPS** are also good to bring along.

Tent Sweet Tent

For many people, home away from home is a tent. Select the right tent for where and when you will be camping. A tent for winter camping should be light but strong. It needs steep walls to keep snow from building up on them. Summer tents should have screens to let in air and keep out bugs. A tent should have a **fly** that fits well to provide airflow and keep rain off your tent walls. There's nothing worse than water in your tent.

Backpackers are more concerned about pack weight than comfort. The more lightweight the tent, the better. You can get a small tent that weighs less than 3 pounds (1.4 kilograms).

GPS—an electronic tool used to find the location of an object; GPS stands for global positioning system

fly—a sheet of material that attaches to a tent for use as a double top or as a rooflike extension

Get Comfy

You can choose from three types of sleeping bags. Mummy style sleeping bags fit tightly around a camper's body. They are the warmest. Semi-rectangular and rectangular bags are roomier.

Different materials are used to make sleeping bags. Cotton sleeping bags are not recommended for serious camping. They're heavy, but they won't keep you as warm or as dry as other bags. Some **synthetic** materials are better because they're waterproof or stay warm when wet. Sleeping bags are filled with down or synthetic fiber **insulation**. Down filling is thicker and warmer than synthetic filling. But down is useless if it gets soggy. Keep these qualities in mind when choosing your sleeping bag.

synthetic—artificial or made by people rather than found in nature

insulation—a material that stops heat or cold from entering or escaping

mummy style sleeping bag

Backpacks

If you will be hiking, a pack that fits well and holds all your gear is a must. Hundreds of pack styles are available. Most hikers use backpacks. Day packs for short trips do not need frames. But when you're carrying a lot of gear, a pack with a frame works best. The frame helps to keep the weight even so you don't have to work as hard.

Some backpacks have lightweight frames inside the pack. Internal frames allow for easy movement. The frame is flexible, so the pack shapes comfortably to your body. Newer models have a "cool space" between the pack and your back to let air flow through.

If you need to carry a lot of gear, you may want an external frame pack. But remember that you can't move as freely with an external frame pack. These packs aren't recommended for skiing or mountain climbing.

All backpacks should have padded shoulder straps and a support belt. A pack for long trips should also have a chest strap. The chest strap keeps shoulder straps in place to balance the weight on your body.

FACT
Put heavy items at the bottom of your pack and lighter items on top. Packing this way will reduce back strain.

Drink Up!

Where you camp determines if you'll need to bring water. Most public campsites provide running water or access to clean water. If you're heading into the wilderness, you need to bring or find your own water. Lake and river water may look clear and clean, but could contain bacteria. But enough water to last a week will be very heavy to carry. Instead of packing water, consider using a water purification system to make lake and river water safe to drink.

If your trip involves easy access to boats, cars, or RVs, you have more room for supplies. You can bring large containers of clean water instead of a purification system. But to be safe, it's a good idea to bring iodine tablets. The tablets dissolve and kill germs in water. This makes lake and river water drinkable in an emergency.

If you're stuck without a purification system or iodine tablets, there's one more way to make water drinkable. Boiling water for one minute will kill germs and bacteria too.

WILD AND WOODSY

Campers going deep into the wilderness need to bring extra equipment.

- An adult can use a hatchet to clear brush or cut firewood.
- A backpacking stove is small enough to carry and allows you to cook without a fire.
- A small shovel can be used to dig a toilet or a safe hollow for a fire.
- Waterproof bags will keep your gear dry.
- Nylon cord can be used to secure a tent and to hang food from a tree.

Cruise and Camp

Driving into a campsite gives you more room for equipment. You could bring a larger cooking surface, such as a grill, cook stove, or Dutch oven. An inflatable mattress or cot will give you more comfort for sleeping. You can even bring a portable toilet if restrooms aren't available at the campground.

RVs are designed to bring all the comforts of home with you. They have small kitchens, beds, and built-in tables. Some also have bathrooms and refrigerators. At an RV campsite, you can hook up your RV to electricity and water.

Many people like to camp with an RV. But don't forget to enjoy nature. A car or RV can carry a large TV. But the point of going camping is to enjoy the wonders of nature. Don't get hooked on the extras!

FACT
Some dogs enjoy camping too. Just make sure to check the rules of the camp area. Most national parks do not allow dogs.

CHAPTER 3

FROM BEAR BAGS TO BANDAGES

For safety, the two rules are preparation and awareness. Ask about the campground rules. Check the weather forecast. Find out what animals are in the area. Thinking ahead and learning all you can will help you have a safe trip.

Bear Bagging

Raccoons, bears, and other animals often crash campsites to find food. Campers should store food and trash away from their sleeping area. Using a hanging storage bag, or bear bag, will keep unwanted guests away. Find a tree at least 100 yards (91 meters) from your campsite. Hang the bag from a branch high enough that animals cannot reach it. In bear country, it's best to even avoid cooking within 100 yards (91 m) of your sleeping area.

FACT
Bear spray is good to have in an emergency. It's like pepper spray that you spray in a bear's face.

Fire Safety

Wildfires destroy forests and put people and animals in danger. Make sure any fire you build is a size you can control. Campfires should be at least 15 feet (4.6 m) away from your tent. Local rules may require fires to be farther away, so be sure to ask. Also, check the area around the fire. Clear brush or low tree branches nearby to keep fire from spreading.

Always make sure your fire is out before you leave a campsite. You can use dirt or water to put out the fire. But with dirt, roots could remain burning under the dirt pile. Using water to put out a fire is best. Pour water over the fire until it stops hissing. Stir the ashes with a shovel to make sure everything is soaked.

First Aid

Having a first-aid kit is essential when you're out in the wilderness. Beyond a standard kit, other items may be useful. If you will be in an area with venomous snakes, include a snakebite kit. Hydrocortisone cream is good to have in case you come across poison ivy, poison oak, or sumac. But having the right supplies is only half the battle. Take a first-aid class before your trip so you're prepared in an emergency.

FIRST-AID KITS

A standard first-aid kit should contain:

- antiseptic wipes
- burn gel
- gauze pads
- adhesive tape
- vinyl gloves
- emergency blanket
- moleskin patches
- adhesive bandages
- pain relievers
- tweezers
- CPR protection mask
- instant cold icepack

CHAPTER 4

WE'RE HERE. NOW WHAT?

The tent is set up. The toilet has been found. All the sleeping bags are unrolled and the cooler has been stowed. What now?

See What You Can See

Camping provides the ideal opportunity to enjoy nature. You can spot animals while just walking through the woods. With binoculars, you can observe animals from a distance. Bring a guidebook with you to see how many plants or animals you can identify.

Near water, you can paddle out in a boat or canoe and wait. Anything from a loon to a muskrat or even a moose could swim by. Many campers also enjoy fishing.

Enjoying nature makes for a great camping trip. Just be sure to stay a safe distance away from all animals, for your safety and theirs.

Treasure Hunting

A compass and map are already necessary equipment for camping. But did you know you can put them to use for fun? Take turns with a friend setting up a scavenger hunt. Place objects in specific places. Then choose a starting point. List how many steps in which direction each object is located. Then use a compass to find them one at a time. If you think it's fun, you might try **geocaching**. It's similar, but uses a portable GPS to find objects hidden by other people.

geocaching—a sport involving finding objects by using a GPS device

The Night Life

Camping provides some downtime too. Evenings offer quality time with friends and family. Many campers enjoy gathering around the campfire. Campfires are great for roasting hot dogs and marshmallows. Some campers tell ghost stories around the fire.

Camping is also a great time to watch the night sky. Most campsites are far away from the lights of the city. See if you can identify the constellations. If you're lucky you may see a meteor shower. If you have enough room, a telescope is a fun addition to your equipment.

CHAPTER 5

LEAVE NO TRACE

Campers should try to have as little impact on nature as possible. This view of camping is called Leave No Trace. It means taking everything you brought into camp out with you. It also means respecting wildlife. Leave No Trace camping also encourages campers to learn to build safe, controlled fires and to plan ahead.

FACT
The Leave No Trace Center for Outdoor Ethics promotes the principles of Leave No Trace and offers education and training.

Leave No Trace promotes camping on existing sites or hard surfaces. It also recommends using existing trails. That way the untouched parts of nature stay untouched.

If you are out in the wild without a toilet, Leave No Trace recommends digging a **cathole**. The cathole should be 200 feet (61 m) away from trails, water, and campsites. Dig 6 to 8 inches (15 to 20 centimeters) into the ground. Then be sure to cover the hole when you're finished using it.

Another point of Leave No Trace is to leave behind anything you find in nature. It can be tempting to bring rocks or feathers home from your trip. But leaving them there allows other campers to enjoy them. If we all pitch in, we can protect nature. Then everyone can enjoy camping in the years to come.

cathole—a small hole in the ground for waste

FUNDING

Much of the funding for state and national parks comes from grants. Fees for camping and hunting permits also help support the parks. Many states also sell conservation license plates to raise money for nature and wildlife preservation.

GLOSSARY

cathole (CAT-hole)—a small pit in the ground for human waste

conservation (kon-sur-VAY-shuhn)—the protection of valuable things, especially forests, wildlife, and natural resources

fly (FLYE)—a sheet of material that attaches to a tent for use as a double top or as a rooflike extension

geocaching (JEE-oh-cash-ing)—a sport involving finding objects by using GPS or compass directions

GPS—an electronic tool used to find the location of an object; GPS stands for global positioning system

grant (GRANT)—a gift such as land or money given for a particular purpose

insulation (in-suh-LAY-shun)—a material that stops heat or cold from entering or escaping

preserve (pri-ZURV)—a place where animals can live and be protected from hunters

synthetic (sin-THET-ik)—artificial or made by people rather than found in nature

READ MORE

Hurley, Michael. *Surviving the Wilderness*. Extreme Survival. Chicago: Raintree, 2011.

Long, Denise. *Survivor Kid: A Practical Guide to Wilderness Survival*. Chicago: Chicago Review Press, 2011.

Mason, Paul. *Hiking and Camping: The World's Top Hikes and Camping Spots*. Passport to World Sports. Mankato, Minn.: Capstone, 2011.

INTERNET SITES

FactHound offers a safe, fun way to find Internet sites related to this book. All of the sites on FactHound have been researched by our staff.

Here's all you do:

Visit *www.facthound.com*

Type in this code: 9781429684231

Super-cool stuff! Check out projects, games and lots more at **www.capstonekids.com**

INDEX